A Monster in a backpack

Contents

The Key maker

"Walls divide spaces, windows show us different spaces, doors allow communication between spaces, locks throw all these equations out of balance, and keys give them meaning again."

The key maker uttered these words as he was making a spare key for the young woman.

The woman said: "I don't feel safe without a lock", took the key from the key maker and left without seeing the immense loneliness the key maker was suffering from.

****

The Red Stain

"It can't get any worse than this."

The man said these words, slammed the door, and walked out of the house.
He repeated the same words over and over again that night.

When he realized the money he had on him was not enough to pay for a hotel room or even a motel,
When he realized he had no friends or family in the big city where he could spend the night,
When he realized that park benches were too cold to spend the night on,
When he realized he had to go back to the house he had left in anger,

He went home and realized his wife had made a huge red stain on the floor with a small slit in her wrist.

That's It?

The man walked to the deep, open well thinking to himself: "It is possible that my impact against the wall of the well will hinder the speed of the fall."

He went to the foot of the tallest tree in the jungle: "It's too bushy and I might get stuck on the branches."

He went to the tallest skyscraper in the city: "This is good. There are no chances of being saved here. Oh how thrilling! And why not something taller than this? I could at least have some fun before dying!"

He started to think: "Finding a rock in the mountains which is taller than skyscrapers is very difficult. Instead, I can go kiting and experience flying as well. I can fly as high as possible and then let go."

And that's what he did. He went kiting and experienced flying. He flew as high as he could, let himself go, and died."

"That's it!?"
"Yes! Were you expecting something else?"

****

The Smilodon

In prehistoric times (more or less 20,000 years ago), a mute man lived in a cave with his mate and small children. He spent his days hunting and returned home at night, with or without a prey. He was so exhausted that he did not even have the energy to mate. One day, he was attacked by a smilodon in the jungle. The mute man had no choice but to tear open the smilodon's chest with his spear. Proud of his victory, he returned home.

He tried to tell his mate what had happened. But as hard as he tried to explain with signs, he was unable to bring home the message. He made a drawing on the cave wall with a sharp stone and boasted his heroic warfare to his mate. He came to realize what a talent he had for painting. Be that as it may, his partner made signs with her hands and said angrily: "So what? What kind of catch is this! Your children are hungry!" The man walked out of the cave angrily. He carried on drawing on every flat rock he could find to spite his mate. All he did was draw. After some time, he went back to the cave again and saw that everyone had starved to death. He could now add creativity to his drawings. This is how he made his drawings this time: The smilodon kills his family and the vengeful man kills the saber-toothed tiger in a bloody battle.

****

The Woodcutter

Once upon a time, a woodcutter went into the forest. He was looking for a dead tree to start his work as per his daily routine. He was about to go deeper into the forest when, all of a sudden, he came across the biggest tree around; a tree so big that a thousand men had to hold hands around it to figure out its circumference. He turned to the big tree and said: "I am a kind, caring man and only cut down dead trees. My love for this forest abounds; but you are big and you boast your greatness to me. Beware that I am god of the forest and it is love that makes a god, not size and magnitude. Know this - a god cannot be incompetent, even when it comes to cutting you down. And know this too - once I've cut you down I won't know right from wrong.

The tree remained silent. Everyone knows trees cannot talk. So, he picked up his axe and began bringing it down on the tree. He thrashed it, and thrashed it, and thrashed it until he was dead.

In later times, the battle between these two turned into a legend among the people. A battle between two gods on earth.

But I interpret this story differently. Paranoid schizophrenia!!!

****

Calmness

A woman can be distraught and confused - when vacuuming (the house is clean); when mincing meat (there is no need for this); when filing her nails (scraping the tip of her finger); when flossing her teeth (her gums bleed).

And a man can be calm and peaceful - when his wife is vacuuming; when his wife is mincing meat; when his wife is filing her nails; when his wife is flossing.

A woman can behave unreasonably - when she stays in the bathroom longer than usual, constantly staring at the razor blade in her hand; or when she is standing on the ledge of the balcony on the fifth floor of the building or higher up.

And a man can be the cause of his wife's unreasonable behaviors - when he is listening to soft music; when he is watching a movie with romantic scenes; or when he is reading a poetry book or love stories.

****

Gravity

"Going around the world has been my long-lasting ambition. I'm old now. There's hardly any time left. I must get going. Truth is I haven't a penny to my name. I'm skint. But that's not a good enough reason to stop me. As you know, the earth rotates around its own axis eastward at a speed of one thousand six hundred and seventy-five kilometres per hour. I can reduce the earth's gravity to zero for myself. I must go to a high place to avoid hitting any surfaces. The Damavand Peak is a good one. This way, I can go around the earth in 24 hours, or shall I say in 23 hours, 56 minutes, and 4 seconds, and return to where I started. But, there is just one point! There are many other mountain ranges in the same latitude as Damavand or the Alborz mountain range! Like the Alps, the Rockies, or the Himalayas. I may be able to pass over the Alps and Rockies, but I'm a little afraid of the

Himalayas. But, it's still not a good enough reason why I shouldn't be able to do it. Maybe I can go higher with the aerodynamic movements of my body or go around the peaks. Anyway, I'll come up with a ploy, because there is no time left! I'm getting older and weaker with each passing day."

The old man began walking to Damavand Peak. I am not sure how he can eliminate gravity either. But he spoke as if he knew what he was doing. In any case, I never saw him again. He probably hit a tall Himalayan peak and died. Or he may have fallen into a Pacific Ocean.

****

Alzheimer's Is Not Always Bad

"The pendulum clock you see belonged to my grandfather. When I got married at twenty, he gave it to me as a wedding gift. It is an antique. The base and frame is khatam work from Isfahan. It is made of ebony, ivory, and silver wires. It's a work of art. The hands are gold-plated silver; the dial is made of silver and so is the clockwork. The pendulums are made of bronze. It told the time for sixty years without any problems. But now, it falls one hour behind in every twenty-four hours. Every night, I went to bed at 11 o'clock and woke up at seven the next morning. It's really strange! I'm not sure why the slowness of the clock has disrupted my sleep. Every night, I go to bed an hour earlier than the night before.

I have even been losing about a kilo a day since the day the clock stopped working properly. What's more, my smoking routine has changed too! I smoke a few more every day without noticing. But, all this set aside, I am becoming more and more forgetful by the minute!

To be sure, I must also add that I wasn't especially keen on the clock, but my wife loved it."

(The old man stares at the clock in stupor, pauses for a few minutes.)

"I remember now. My wife passed away on the day the clock broke down."
"Alright! Very well! This is what I wanted to get to! How did she die?"

(The old man goes quiet for a little.)

"The pendulum clock you see belonged to my grandfather. When I got married at twenty…"

****

Liberation

I must start with my room. I need a large litterbag, which I don't have. I have to throw away everything in the room. The sculpture I didn't make; the painting I didn't draw; the story I didn't write; the poem I didn't recite. I have thrown everything into the litterbag, which I don't have. Right, let's get to the larger stuff now. For instance, the double bed I don't have; or the closet with all the clothes in it, which I don't have. I also throw all those in the litterbag that I don't have. There is nothing special left in the room anymore. I have thrown everything in the hallway, sitting room, and kitchen in the litterbag, which I don't have. I leave the house. I who have nothing but the house I don't have. So, I throw the house in the litterbag I don't have. Oh! I completely forgot! What will happen to the wife I don't have and the children I don't have! Cause, I don't have the heart to throw them in the litterbag that I don't have too! But it can't be helped. I have to. I also throw them in the litterbag that I don't have.

What a large volume of stuff! I can't carry it all. I leave it behind in the street and walk away.

And now, I place the cardboard that I do have on the pavement that I do have and go to sleep on it. I have no more attachments. Liberation is a good feeling, if you are not hungry!

****

The Hunter

I was fourteen. We had a mud hut near the Aras River. Our nearest neighbor lived a few miles away from us. I had a father and a mother, and seven sisters.

My father was a hunter. Whenever we came across a fox or a jackal, he used to say: "A hunter doesn't shoot another hunter." My father always used to make such comments, and I never had the nerve to ask him the reason why.

As I was hunting partridges, I noticed two black wolves on the next hill. The wolves saw me too, eye to eye. Although they were within firing range, I didn't shoot them. Not because of my father's comments. I like wolves. Wolves are brave and unafraid.

I was very afraid of my father. He was moody and short-tempered. I never heard my father laugh. In reality, not a day went by when he didn't raise his hand on my mother and sisters. Perhaps he wanted mother to give him more sons. And this was the reason behind his perpetual sourness and rancor with her. He hit her for no reason at all. I probably suffered more than my mother and sisters did. Father came home on a snowy day. He turned to mother and said: "Ayāz Khan wants Jeiran. Get her ready for tomorrow morning. I'll take her to him."

Ayāz Khan was the headman of the village next door. He was a heavily built man just like father and an old friend of his. Father was also keen to be related to Ayāz Khan.
Jeiran was a year younger than me. I also had three sisters who were older than Jeiran. But Ayāz Khan had an eye out for Jerian's beauty. Father told me to accompany him the following day.

Jeiran was crying at bedtime. I know why.

Come the next day, all three of us set out for the village. It was snowing. Father and I took a rifle each. He walked ahead of us and Jeiran and I followed a few steps behind. Strong winds were blowing in the snowstorm. Our eyes could only see the whiteness of the snow. I wanted to stop father and say but why? Ayāz Khan already has four wives and fourteen concubines! What does he want with Jeiran? But I couldn't. They always say cowards die a thousand deaths, that fear is the brother of death. I wish I had been courageous enough.

We were on our way when I felt that we had fellow travelers. The path was lined with poplar trees and tall grass. It was tough to see who was traveling with us. Jeiran had covered her face with a few scarves to keep the freezing cold out. There was nothing around. I threw a glance behind me. Two black wolves were following us a few steps away. They had paced themselves with us. I should have been scared and ran off. Yet, I'm not quite sure why the presences of the two wolves with their frightening faces put me at ease. I had a feeling they were the same two wolves I had seen previously. I felt no fear or apprehension. I turned around and looked straight ahead as if nothing had happened. Jeiran was oblivious. So was my father. We took a few more steps together. I thought maybe it was a figment of my imagination. I looked back again. There was no doubt about it. I saw the wolves. I grabbed Jeiran's hand and we both stopped. Both wolves trotted past us. Jeiran was about to scream as she saw them, but I placed my hand over her mouth to keep her quiet. The wolves attacked my father from behind and tore him apart. I took my hand off Jeiran's mouth. She said: "Don't you have a rifle!? Shoot the wolves!"

I said: "A hunter doesn't shoot another hunter."

****

The End

He lied down on the bed, closed his eyes, and whispered to himself.

"A cottage on the forest hill with a walnut tree and stables next to it; a farm downstream where food can grow; letting chickens, roosters, ducks, geese, turkeys, and a few heads of cows and bulls roam around the forest. Go eat as much grass as you can find on this rotating circle and return to the stables at sunset to my herding calls of "hey, hey". A river runs along the farm. You just have to throw in a fishing line and catch rainbow trout. At night, you can lie down on the portico away from these synthetic lights and observe the moonlight and stars. In the morning, you can wake up to the sound of the woodpeckers pecking on the trunk of the walnut tree or the sensational song of eagles in the sky. Breakfast, lunch, and dinner…"

The door of the room flings open. Two soldiers walk the prisoner to the gallows.

****

Pests as Neighbors

The walls of my home are so thin that when the neighbors on both sides of our flat turn on their television sets, the sound travels from the neighbor's flat on the right to the neighbor's flat on the left, and from the neighbor's flat on the left to the neighbor's flat on the right. Just imagine the state of my flat in the middle of these two. I have no television but I am constantly listening to the sound of my neighbors' televisions with great interest. The interesting part is that they both love horror movies; nonsensical screenplay conversations that "the devil is reincarnated in me" and "nonstop screaming", and so on.

To begin with, I was curious and interested and followed the sounds with great pleasure. But then, I began to get jittery. Everyone has to feel relaxed in their own home. You can't relax with the neighbors making this much noise. I have to let them know not to disturb my peace. I might also add that you cannot make your neighbors respect your rights by bullying them. It will surely lead to bad feelings. I must do it calmly in a friendly manner. I took a box of chocolates as a gift and went to my neighbor on the left. I knocked on the door and the neighbor opened it. I realized I had made a mistake as soon as I set eyes on him. I apologized and went home quickly. I put the box of chocolates on the table and scratched my hand with a razor blade. I poured a few drops of blood in a glass and went back to the neighbor's flat. He accepted my gift. We chatted for a while and then I returned home. He was a good neighbor. But I never went to see my other neighbor.

****

Death

He woke up suddenly, among thousands of dead! He thought he was dead too. But seemingly, he was still alive and there was still hope. He tried to think of a ploy, but to no avail. He could not breathe. He was suffocating. He had very little time left. They were shoveling up the dead on top of one another. He lost all hope. But, he got a stroke of unexpected luck! As they were piling up the dead, he ended up on top of the pile. He was so close to the edge of the platform. He could now save himself with a little effort. He just had to move his spine like a resilient spring. That is what he did and fell into the water.

Suddenly, a shark came along and swallowed the fish.

****

The Game Club

A man who loved crossword puzzles knew very well that puzzles generated no income. Ergo, he became a president.

Every single world leader was invited to the headquarters of the General Assembly of the United Nations. Following extensive talks, they realized that all the presidents, depending on their culture and the geography of their country, loved games such as Sudoku, chess, backgammon, and traditional games all in all. Some of the advanced countries also loved digital games like Call of Duty and God of War. The presidents of certain developing countries were busy with similar digital games but with a lower quality, like Bomber Man and Super Mario.
The presidents got into an argument about which game was the best. The crossword puzzle

which added to your general knowledge, the Sudoku which developed mental math abilities, games that inject vitality into people, games that teach humans war tactics, or chess which models political strategies!?

Eventually, the Secretary-General of the United Nations issued a statement with the consensus of all the presidents, stating:

> The headquarters of the UN General Assembly must be converted into a well-equipped gaming club (whether traditional or digital). All presidents are required to attend the club twelve times a year, for a period of four weeks every time and play with the other presidents.

And thus, lasting peace took shape worldwide.

****

Adrenalin

The 120-year-old man paid no attention to the 20-year-old man who was the safety office for bungee jumping who was saying: "You are not allowed to do this activity at your age!"

And the old man was saying: "Which law sets out the age conditions? I have read the regulations. I have no heart disease! I'm over the age of fourteen! I weigh less than ninety kilos! And I have never been to the doctor's in the last 100 years. This means I am in perfect health!"

The safety officer wanted to ask the old man to sit down for a few minutes and glance over the safety rules. But as hard as he searched, he found no case! So, he was forced to give the old man permission to go ahead. He started tying the elastic rope around his ankles, followed by the fall from the tower. When he heard the old man shouting in excitement, he knew he was alright.

When it was over, he pulled up the old man with great relief; but what he saw was very different from what he had seen earlier. The old man was no longer old. He had turned into a 20-year-old man.

The safety officer was reviewing the incident in bewilderment. How could this be possible!?

The rejuvenated old man said: "I must see what exciting things will be invented in the next 100 years so I can try them too."

****

The Shroud Maker

It is said that tailors are in cahoots with witches.
So, I went to a tailor and asked: "Is this true?"
The tailor said: "Is what true?"
I said: "Wishes."
The tailor said: "Yes, but it has nothing to do with witchcraft. Imagine you wish to be a rich man! Wear his clothes. Then, riches will come to you."
I said: "I'm not after riches. I want to see my love."
The tailor said: "It makes no difference. Wear the clothes your love likes. If you don't know what that is, then you must know that the person is not your love."

I thought for a while, and said: "I want a burial shroud, like the one my love is wearing. Can you make one for me?"

****

Extinction

My parents did not know why I was born. I told them: "If you don't answer my question today, I'll kill you!" (My parents laughed.)

These words were uttered by a 4-year-old boy.

In later years, he tried to annihilate humankind. It would suffice for him to escape the educational and correctional nucleus.

****

Enters the Commissar

And quietly leaves through the backdoor

Commissar : Did you murder the victim?

Maid : I was washing the master's clothes. I had no idea that he was going to a party. I think he had a date with the girl. I don't know; there is no fool like an old fool. It's really none of my business. I just made a few pennies to pay for my daughter's dowry. I'm out of work now. Do you know where I can find a job?

Commissar : What about you?

Gardener : I was in the garden. I was tilling the flowerbeds with a shovel. The master enjoyed the scent of roses. I wanted to plant some for him next to the fence. By the way, do you know anyone who's looking for a gardener? My wife is sick! How am I supposed to pay for her medicine?

Commissar : What about you? Where were you when the murder happened?

Personal Driver: Nowhere! I was in a foul mood. I went out to get some cigarettes! I have two brats at school. First and second grades. They need books, notebooks. My daughter will start school next year too! And I'm out of a job! Damn this life. I wanted to ask the master for an advance on next month's pay. And now he's said his goodbyes.

Commissar : What were you doing?

Cook : Well, I thought to myself now that the master is going out to dinner tonight I could tidy the kitchen a bit and go home, because my mother is home all by herself. She's old. She can't walk. I thought I could be with her for tonight at least. I don't know night from day anymore,

and now I've no more work. May
God help me.

The commissar had to complete his last case file
so he could retire. He had no more patience for
questioning the suspects. All he could think of
was who to blame for the murder.

****

The Scarab Beetle

He abhorred the disgusting smell of dung.
His mother said: "This is the way of our forefathers. You have to accept it."

He always said: "I'd like to barbecue worms on the fire! Or become a vegetarian altogether! Why do you block my progress?"

Mother slapped him and objected with a tut-tut to his son talking contrary to customs!

She always said: "Wait until your father gets home to give you a good talking to!"
He was terrified of his father. He collected his bric-a-brac in a bag and left the house at night.
When hunger found him, he tasted every plant around and spit them out instantly. He had no idea how bad plants could taste.

He started hunting for worms. He made a fire and cooked the worms. He sampled them, but they tasted so bad he spat them out too.

He was sad and depressed. He had to go home and apologize to his parents. He went into the house. This time, his father treated him kindly and took him in his arms, saying: "It's good that you went away and saw how things are with your own eyes. Now you know that there is a good reason for the way of our forefathers. This is the essence of us scarab beetles, whether good or bad. Now go sleep and I'll see you tomorrow."

He went and laid down. He was not sleepy. He thought about the philosophy behind this injustice until the break of dawn, but to no avail.

He woke up with sleepy eyes the next morning. Tired, he began rolling the dung!

Footnote: Swedish scientists have discovered that scarab beetles map their route according to the Milky Way. It must be our own little scarab beetle who has found a way to do this. We must keep an eye out for his other discoveries.

****

Backgammon

I must go to the shelter. The world is not a safe place for me! I might have an accident on the street, or in the elevator which may collapse any minute; the bridge might collapse while I'm on it, or lightning might strike. Worse still, a meteorite might hit me right smack in the fontanelle. Even a whirlwind could pick up everything under the sky and in the sea, like fish, fruits, trees, automobiles, kayaks, boats, skyscrapers, and mountains, and drop it all on my unfortunate head.

Now, you might ask why I think I am so unlucky? I will tell you and you can be the judge.

Yesterday, I was playing backgammon with one of my friends. I was a beginner, but as my bad luck would have it the dice categorically refused to play along with me.

Depression

The umbrella is always over my head, even if it is raining diamonds from the sky. It makes no difference.

I will now change the problem. You are sitting on a park bench and it is going to rain a beautiful girl. Would you like her to be in your arms or fall on the umbrella?

Under the circumstances, I prefer to turn my umbrella upside down.

****

The Train

I picked up my backpack and set out for the train station. I had no set destination. I am a person who never makes any plans. Of course, I'll never condone it. We all must determine our destination in advance. But at that time, I had to go to the train station first and choose my destination once there; because I am a person who never makes any plans. I glanced at the train schedule. It was eight in the morning. All the trains for Tabriz, Bandar Abbas, Rasht, and so forth, were full. The only train with one seat available was headed to the abyss. It was leaving in a few minutes. I did not know much about the abyss. I asked the ticket seller: Is the abyss a tourist destination? He said he had no accurate information on the place but could ask the passengers headed there.

I bought my ticket and got on the train. It reeked of corpses. Of course, I should have known. A train of dead passengers must of course reek of corpses. I was unable to enter my compartment for the foul smell. I went to the restaurant and pulled a window down a little to get some fresh air and feel better. I was waiting for the waiter when the ticket controller walked in and glanced at me. He paused for a second, took my ticket, and punched it.

He said: "You do know that this is a no-return train?"
I said: "I didn't know. But I'm glad you told me."
He said: "How come the ticket seller didn't inform you?"
I said: "I don't know. Maybe because I had died before I was dead!"

****

A Coffee Reading

The woman who did the coffee readings arrived at the coffee shop. She was looking for a prey to fool. She saw a young man sitting on chair with a doleful expression on his face. There was no ring on his finger and his clothes were crumpled up. But a wallet and car keys sat at a table, meaning he was financially fit. She walked up to him and offered to tell his fortune. The man shook his head as a sign of acceptance.

The woman fortune teller took a look at the remaining coffee grounds in the cup and said: "You are a lucky man. I can see a magician. It means your future success will dazzle all eyes. I also see an eagle; this is a gift of pride and honor bestowed by the universe. Aren't you lucky! This here shows a path. It means you have to choose the right path. There is a little boat in this corner. It means if you choose the wrong path, you needn't worry at all. You can still return; it just delays you a little. Chrysanthemums are also..."

The fortune teller was about to show the chrysanthemum as a sign of fiery love when the man quickly stood up happy with his reading and paid her over the amount she was asking for.

The man went to his car and drove off to the factory from where he has just been fired. On the way there, he stopped at a knife store and purchased a large switchblade.

****

The Job Interview

"Education?"
"Master of Mortality Development"
"Experience?"
"I have been mostly in Africa. My working method included hunger and thirst."
 "Reason for leaving your last job?"
"I was sacked. There was talk of laxity, but I did not agree at all."
"Fill in the form and wait outside. Also, call the next person."
#
"Education?"
"PhD in massacre, infectious diseases."
"Experience?"

"I was mostly in East Asia, mainly active in clinics and hospitals."

"Reason for termination?"

"I was sent to Europe on a mission to monitor chemical and microbial bombs. Once my mission was completed, I came to see you. I believe I can add to my experience in different locations."

"Fill in the form and wait outside. Also, ask the next person to come in."

#

"Education?"

"Master in killing civilians"

"Experience?"

"I was mostly in the Middle East."

"Reasons for termination?"

"You may not like my answer. The fact is, I felt sorry for a little girl once. That's why I was sacked! But I assure you it won't happen again. I promise."

"That's OK. Fill in this form and wait outside. Also, ask the next person to come it."

#

"Education?"

"Master of mass killings with nuclear and hydrogen bombs."

47

"Experience?"

"I worked only twice, in Hiroshima and Nagasaki."

"Reason for termination?"

"There have been no mass killings as such for a while. I was made redundant. But, I've heard something is happening. Is that true?"

"No questions. Fill in this form quickly while I talk to the director."

#

"Sir, four people have come for the interview and filled in forms. What are your orders?"

"I think there is no more time. Hire anyone who comes. Place two wings on their shoulders and spread them across the planet. They must wait for my orders. I want them to wrap up the job in the shortest possible time. You have heard the news that Israfil's[1] trumpet has been transferred to earth, haven't you!?"

****

---

1 - is the angel who blows into the trumpet to signal Qiyamah (the Day of Judgment) and sometimes depicted as the angel of music

Gando[2]

There was a little boy called Lalu in Bahukalat village. Lalu was a hunter with a slingshot. All kinds of birds like partridges, francolins, doves, greenfinch, cockers, Baluch squirrels, lizards, and all manner of birds, reptiles, and mammals were killed with a throw of his stone. He hunted, not for himself but for Gando.

He always hunted the right amount. He weighed his prey in his hand by moving it up and down to make sure it was two and a half to three kilograms. Gando did not eat more than that.

2- Gando is the word for the mugger crocodile in the Baluch dialect of southeastern Iran. Their habitat is mainly in Bahukalat village in Sistan-Baluchistan Province.

He had named the Gando; he called it Kukan. It was strong and the name was becoming. The gandos all looked the same to other people. But Lalu always recognized Kukan. Kukan was old and big. When Lalu threw the prey on the ground, Kukan slowly moved towards it and feasted on its nourishment. It was Lalu's turn then. He would lie back to back on Kukan and every tourist who had come hoping to see the crocodiles, aghast with Lalu's boldness, would put their hand in their pocked and throw a few pennies into his bowl – which Lalu had placed at their feet - for the pleasure of having witnessed this breathtaking moment. Lalu was the breadwinner of the family.

Time went by like this until the government came and banned Lalu from doing his work. They placed a guard next to the crocodiles to prevent anyone from getting close.

Lalu was sad. He looked at Kukan with sorrowful eyes and started home. A few days passed until, one night, he heard the sound of the knocker on the door. He opened the door and saw Kukan holding the dead body of a baby Gando in its mouth. It had torn the baby Gando's stomach with its teeth. Kukan slowly placed the victim's body on the doormat and returned towards the marsh.

Big Dirt

One day, big dirt arrived at a small village in a pristine area with a pleasant climate. Big dirt had traveled a long distance from the city and smelled of foul sweat. It had not been relieved himself at all during his trip, so he asked the villagers where the public baths and sanitary facilities were. The inhabitants informed him that no such facilities existed in the village and said big dirt could go to their homes and use their private bathrooms. Big dirt replied that he was not in need of the villagers' hospitality and set out for the river that crossed nearby. As soon as it reached the river, it was no longer able to hold it in and defecated right there and then. Big dirt was so big that his constipated stool created a large dam on the riverbed. Next thing you know, he proceeded to get naked and started taking a bath in the dam it had created. From the dirt stuck on its skin, big dirt was able to build a dirt villa in the dam enclosure. Next to it, he constructed a dirt restaurant, a dirt hotel, and dirt pleasure boats. Then, he began promoting tourism for visitors to come to Dirt Recreational Center and dump all their dirt in this pristine dirt area and its beautiful dirt nature.

****

The Wait

The kettle was always boiling on the cooker with a teapot on top. She kept checking it to make sure the volume of water did not drop due to evaporation. The old woman was waiting for a man whom she knew would come to her house any day now.

It was the middle of the night when the old woman heard a sound and woke up in the bedroom. She went to the window of the room. She was happy. The wait was over. She did not turn the lights on. She wanted to surprise him. The man opened the door and took slow steps towards the room. He did not want to wake the old woman. The old woman was standing behind the curtain with a big grin on her face, waiting to surprise him. The man walked into the bedroom. He was looking for something. The old woman came out from behind the curtain and stood in the doorway. In an abrupt move, she began letting out monstrous screams and evil laughs. The man turned around and stared at the old woman in horror. The old woman threw the boiling water in the kettle in the man's face. He left the house wailing.

Satisfied with a job well done, the old woman went into the room, opened her wooden chest and looked into it joyfully.

****

The Warning Sign

I was driving aimlessly on a road far away from the city. When I say aimlessly, it must not create negative connotations. I have always been aimless in life and enjoyed it too. Like right now, when I don't know where I'm headed or what my route is. But I'm excited, because I know I'll enjoy it and I will never encounter obstacles along the way or fall at the first hurdle, like right this minute that I have reached a fork. The signpost has no indication of destination and is just a warning sign. To the left: Danger of Satan falling, to the right: danger of Azrael falling. Well, it is perfectly clear! If I fork right, I may die and miss out on the joys of life. And then again, I might not; but I have no knowledge about life after death. I take no chances and fork left. What could Satan possibly do? I am focused on the space above. If I see him falling, I'll do a zigzag.

As I was moving on the left fork, Satan fell abruptly at high speed and blocked the way. I was lucky not to hit it and managed to do an emergency stop. I never imagined him to be so fast and so huge. It came towards me with an angry look. As it got a little closer, he changed his angry look to a sarcastic smile and said: Are you the one who lives aimlessly?
I said: Yes
He laughed and said: Right! So I don't need to fool you. Carry on living aimlessly until Azrael finds you.

****

The Apology

Everywhere in the world, it is customary to apologize when you are wrong. But it is said that the Japanese apologize even after every good deed they do. For instance, when they say hello or goodbye, after an invention, or when others give them encouragement, and even before committing kamikaze.[3]

Certainly this behavior is a product of the pure Japanese culture which they have acquired throughout their ancient history.

---

3 - Kamikaze is a Shinto (god's way) word meaning "divine wind". It refers to the suicide missions of the Imperial Japanese Army Air Force against allied forces.

If only this culture was important for my country too so that I could drop thousands of apology letters over the people of Hiroshima and Nagasaki before dropping the atomic bomb.

The Iron

He woke up and walked to the bathroom. As he was taking a shower he remembered that he had a briefing with the head of the department about a verbal and a little physical conflict he had had with a client. He left his shower unfinished, got dressed angrily, and went to the office. He must tell the head of department that he was unable to meet any clients and had to be transferred to another section where he could have no contact until the end of the working day. On his way to the office, he kept thinking that he has to use the same angry face as per usual so that his boss could not contradict him.

He arrived at the office. His colleagues looked at him in surprise when they saw him. He paid no attention because he was angry. He went to his boss's office and wasted no time telling him what was on his mind.

Surprised, the boss told him: Why do look like an electric iron?

The employee turned towards the glass which looked almost like a mirror and said: Yes, you are right.

The boss answered coolly: Never mind. We have absolutely no such position in this office. It would not have made any difference even if we did. I am firing you according to regulation.

The employee blew his top at hearing the word fire, burning his temperature control knob and heating element beyond repair.

****

Bacteria

At a meeting with managers and workers, the highway project director said: I am sorry to say that I am not feeling well at the moment. I will make it short and sweet. By purchasing a tunnel boring machine, tunneling will be carried out easily and in the shortest possible time without requiring drilling and blasting. With a circular cross section, the boring machine will excavate a tunnel with a diameter of twelve meters and provide the best way for you dear colleagues to work. Therefore, we are hoping to deliver the project in about sixty days with the good cooperation of the site manager and other engineers.

After his short speech, the project manager got into his car and drove to the hospital. He managed to find his doctor despite the state he was in.

The doctor said: I am very sorry to say the news is not good. The test results show a type of bacteria which have circular cross sections and drill holes in your body. They feed on your flesh and come out the other end. Some also explode inside you due to a combination of gases and chemical elements. They are about twelve microns in diameter and will kill you in an estimated sixty-day period. Sadly, there is no cure for it.

****

A Monster in a Backpack

There was a 7-year-old girl in whose backpack lived a huge monster. The monster never scared anyone. He was very bashful and his only problem was that he was hungry all the time. The little girl had to constantly feed him everything in the fridge and kitchen cabinets and yet the monster complained of hunger the whole time. The girl was always nervous and angry both for her monster's great appetite and her parent's nonstop arguments.

One day, when she came home from school, she saw her mother sitting on the sofa with a bruise under her mouth. The girl did not say anything; neither did her mother. She went to her room and opened up her backpack. The monster had opened his mouth again, indicating that he was still hungry. She told the monster: "I have nothing for you to eat" and she stretched out on her bed. The monster kept tossing and turning and banging against the walls. The girl got so mad that she took the monster in her hands, looked at it in anger and hatred, opened her mouth so wide at once that she was able to swallow the monster whole.

She went to school the next day and every time someone mocked her for her plumpness, she punched them in the mouth.